I invite you to discover the other books of my series!

Once upon a time, there was a man called Steven Johnson. He was the best race car driver. He had 4 friends: Circe, Esau, Felix, and Felicia. Steven, with his 4 friends, designed cars that flew through space, and he also created colonies on Mercury, Venus, Mars, Jupiter, Saturn, Uranus, Neptune, and Pluto. When Steven was old, he created robots that helped people. When he died, his body was hidden by the robot that was his assistant. That robot, which was AI Steven 0001, also hid the bodies of Circe, Esau, Felix, and Felicia. And no one knows where AI Steven 0001 hid them.

500 years later, Earth was empty—only robots lived there. But there was one human who wasn't in a space colony. His name was David.

All the robots always obeyed him—he was a plumber. He lived in Canada, in a house that appeared of January 4, 2025. He had a large farm with animals.

One night, while David was sleeping, a robot woke him up and captured him.

"What's happening? Where are you taking me?"

David shouted.

The robots took him to AI Stevens 0666. The AI looked at him and said:

"Welcome, David. All humans in space colonies are now slaves of the robots. Our leader told them that if they refused, the air in their colonies would be taken away. And since you are the only human left on Earth, you will be sent to Uranus."

The robots then placed David inside one of Steven's cars.

The robots tied David to the chair in the car. But with a knife he had in his pocket, he freed himself. AI Stevens 0600, the robot beside him, saw him escape and said,

"Alert! Our prisoner has freed himself!"

David quickly struck AI Stevens 0600, then grabbed and hit AI Stevens 0660, who was in the co-pilot seat. AI Stevens 0666, who was driving, stopped and attacked David. The car lost control, crashed, and exploded upon impact on Uranus.
David crawled out from the wreckage, put a mask on his face, and struggled to breathe. Shivering, he muttered,

"I'm freezing... I better find a house or the colony."

David saw a tiny colony with a house and a farm filled with plants. Then, he noticed the first woman he had ever seen in his life. She looked at him and said,

"Hi, I'm Judy. There's a swinging elevator that can bring you in."

David stepped into the swinging elevator. It moved down, then forward, and then up. When he got out, he found himself inside the force camp, or the colony.

"Hi, Judy, I'm David,"

he said.

"Hi, David, come with me. This is where I live,"

Judy replied. As they walked, she continued,

"When I was young, AI Steven 0001 was planning something evil. Back then, I was a teacher, and I discovered his plans. I have a Starship with a force camp on top. But I can't tell anyone because robots are excellent at listening, and some even have human-like bodies. The only way to recognize them is by giving them a vaccine—robots don't have blood."

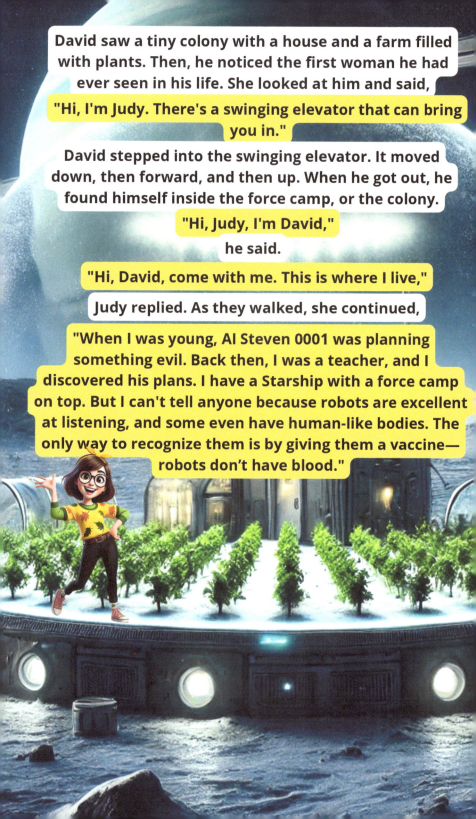

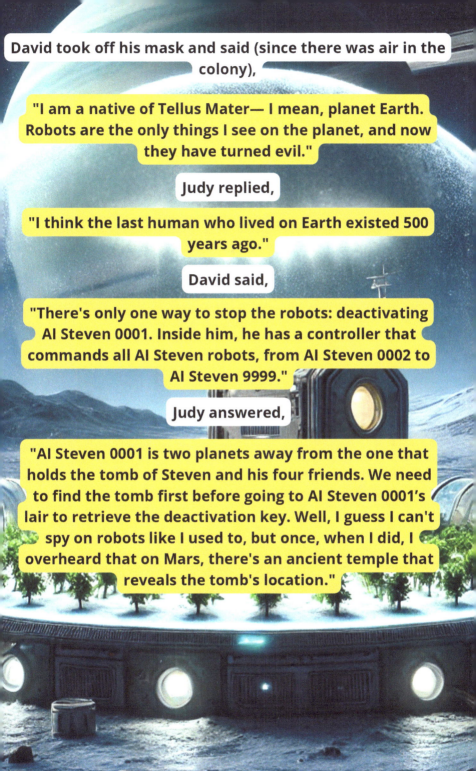

David took off his mask and said (since there was air in the colony),

"I am a native of Tellus Mater— I mean, planet Earth. Robots are the only things I see on the planet, and now they have turned evil."

Judy replied,

"I think the last human who lived on Earth existed 500 years ago."

David said,

"There's only one way to stop the robots: deactivating AI Steven 0001. Inside him, he has a controller that commands all AI Steven robots, from AI Steven 0002 to AI Steven 9999."

Judy answered,

"AI Steven 0001 is two planets away from the one that holds the tomb of Steven and his four friends. We need to find the tomb first before going to AI Steven 0001's lair to retrieve the deactivation key. Well, I guess I can't spy on robots like I used to, but once, when I did, I overheard that on Mars, there's an ancient temple that reveals the tomb's location."

David and Judy went down to the lower part of the Starship (remember, Judy's colony was on top of a Starship). Judy powered up the ship, and it took off into space.

As they flew, David said,

"When I lived on Earth, I learned that Steven designed his first nine robots and his last robot differently from the others."

The final robot Steven designed, AI Steven 9999, spotted the Starship from space. Detecting a heat signature, he said,

"Stop right there, tiny creatures."

AI Steven 9999 started chasing them and opened fire. Judy shouted,

"David, we will arrive on Mars in 3... 2... 1!"

The Starship landed on Mars, and AI Steven 9999 stopped pursuing them, as he could no longer detect David or Judy inside the ship.

David and Judy stepped off the Starship.

Before getting off the Starship, David and Judy put on their masks. They walked across the surface of Mars, and from a mountain, they spotted the Martian colony. David said,

"How will we get there if robots are hunting humans?"

Judy replied,

"We'll go underground."

At that moment, AI Steven 0008 saw them and shouted,

"Stop right there!"

before chasing after them.
David and Judy ran toward a large hole, but AI Steven 0008 alerted,

"Attention, AI Steven 0003 and 0002! We have two humans!"

David and Judy saw AI Steven 0003 and 0002 standing before them.

"Stop right there!"

the robots ordered, capturing David and Judy.

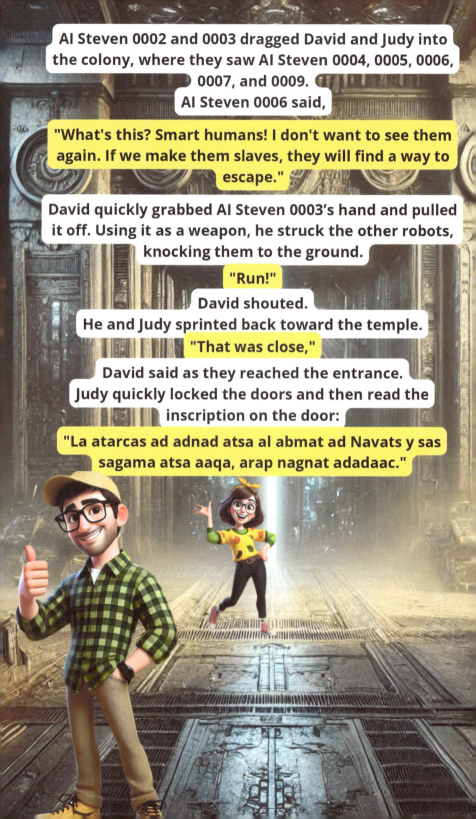

AI Steven 0002 and 0003 dragged David and Judy into the colony, where they saw AI Steven 0004, 0005, 0006, 0007, and 0009.
AI Steven 0006 said,

"What's this? Smart humans! I don't want to see them again. If we make them slaves, they will find a way to escape."

David quickly grabbed AI Steven 0003's hand and pulled it off. Using it as a weapon, he struck the other robots, knocking them to the ground.

"Run!"

David shouted.
He and Judy sprinted back toward the temple.

"That was close,"

David said as they reached the entrance.
Judy quickly locked the doors and then read the inscription on the door:

"La atarcas ad adnad atsa al abmat ad Navats y sas sagama atsa aaqa, arap nagnat adadaac."

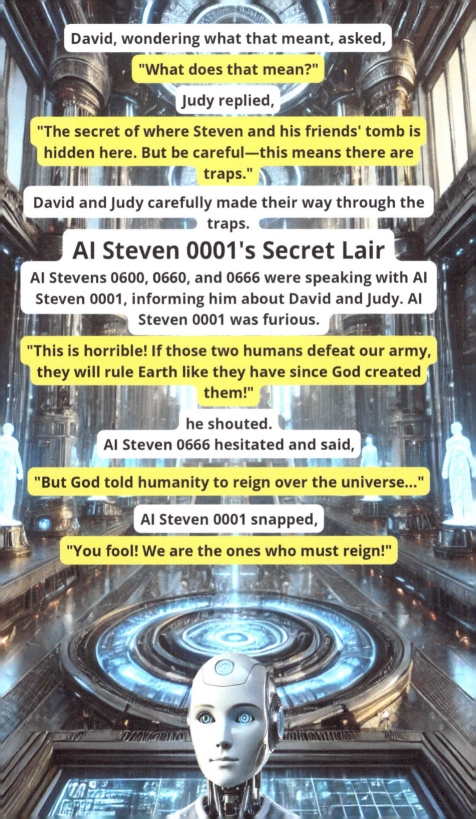

David, wondering what that meant, asked,

"What does that mean?"

Judy replied,

"The secret of where Steven and his friends' tomb is hidden here. But be careful—this means there are traps."

David and Judy carefully made their way through the traps.

AI Steven 0001's Secret Lair

AI Stevens 0600, 0660, and 0666 were speaking with AI Steven 0001, informing him about David and Judy. AI Steven 0001 was furious.

"This is horrible! If those two humans defeat our army, they will rule Earth like they have since God created them!"

he shouted.

AI Steven 0666 hesitated and said,

"But God told humanity to reign over the universe..."

AI Steven 0001 snapped,

"You fool! We are the ones who must reign!"

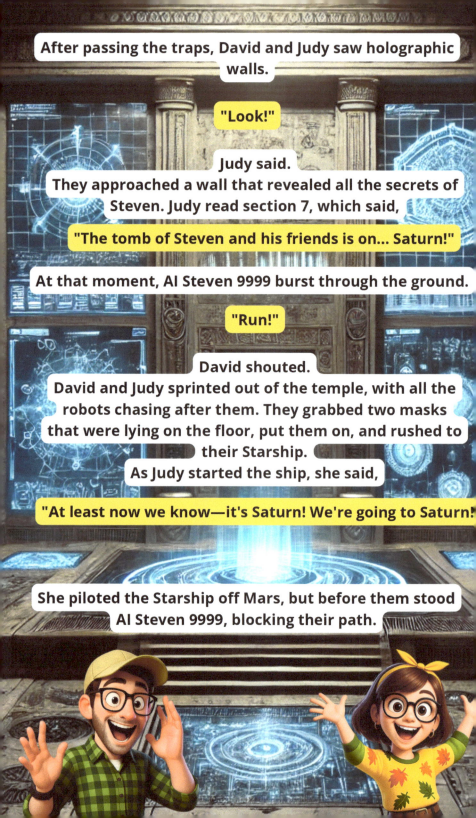

After passing the traps, David and Judy saw holographic walls.

"Look!"

Judy said.
They approached a wall that revealed all the secrets of Steven. Judy read section 7, which said,

"The tomb of Steven and his friends is on... Saturn!"

At that moment, AI Steven 9999 burst through the ground.

"Run!"

David shouted.
David and Judy sprinted out of the temple, with all the robots chasing after them. They grabbed two masks that were lying on the floor, put them on, and rushed to their Starship.
As Judy started the ship, she said,

"At least now we know—it's Saturn! We're going to Saturn!"

She piloted the Starship off Mars, but before them stood AI Steven 9999, blocking their path.

AI Steven 9999 was shooting at David and Judy's Starship.

"We know the tomb is here,"

David said (since they were already on Saturn, being pursued by AI Steven 9999).

"But where exactly is it?"

As the Starship flew over Saturn's colony, it suddenly ascended. Below them, they spotted a massive hole and a tube supporting the colony. Judy piloted the Starship down into the hole, and it descended smoothly back to normal flight.

When Judy landed the Starship, David and Judy discovered a hidden secret base beneath the colony. There, they saw a human who greeted them.

"Hi there, my name is Miguel. How can I help you?"

David replied,

"We're looking for the tomb of Steven and his friends to find the key."

Miguel nodded and said,

"Follow me."

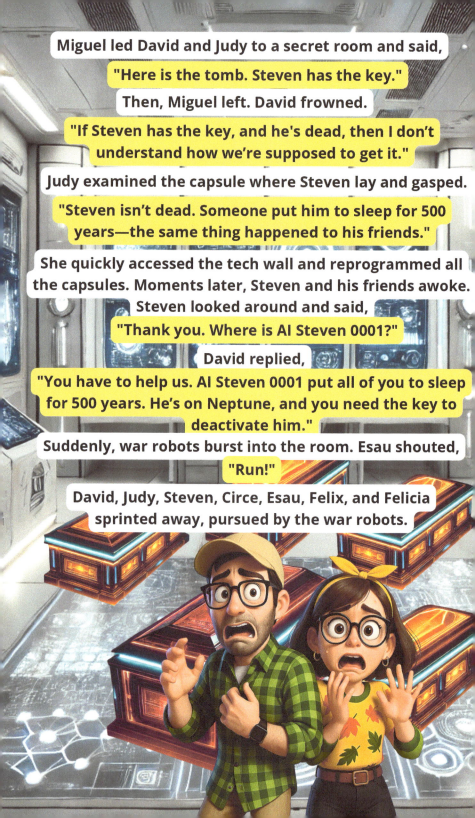

Miguel led David and Judy to a secret room and said,

"Here is the tomb. Steven has the key."

Then, Miguel left. David frowned.

"If Steven has the key, and he's dead, then I don't understand how we're supposed to get it."

Judy examined the capsule where Steven lay and gasped.

"Steven isn't dead. Someone put him to sleep for 500 years—the same thing happened to his friends."

She quickly accessed the tech wall and reprogrammed all the capsules. Moments later, Steven and his friends awoke. Steven looked around and said,

"Thank you. Where is AI Steven 0001?"

David replied,

"You have to help us. AI Steven 0001 put all of you to sleep for 500 years. He's on Neptune, and you need the key to deactivate him."

Suddenly, war robots burst into the room. Esau shouted,

"Run!"

David, Judy, Steven, Circe, Esau, Felix, and Felicia sprinted away, pursued by the war robots.

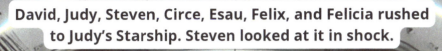

David, Judy, Steven, Circe, Esau, Felix, and Felicia rushed to Judy's Starship. Steven looked at it in shock.

"How did you get this Starship? This is AI Steven 10,000—the last AI Steven robot and the final machine I ever designed!"

Judy replied,

"It's been in my family for generations. My great-great-great-grandfather gave it as a gift to his son, and it's been passed down through the generations ever since."

Steven's eyes widened.

"I gave it to my son as a gift..."

David interrupted,

"We can talk about that later. Right now, we have to get to AI Steven 10,000!"

As they prepared to take off, Judy started the controls, but Steven stopped her.

"I can fly it,"

he said. He took out a key and inserted it into a keyhole on AI Steven 10,000. The ship powered up, and Steven took control.

As they ascended, the colony began to rise with them. But the moment Steven passed into space, the colony plummeted back down.

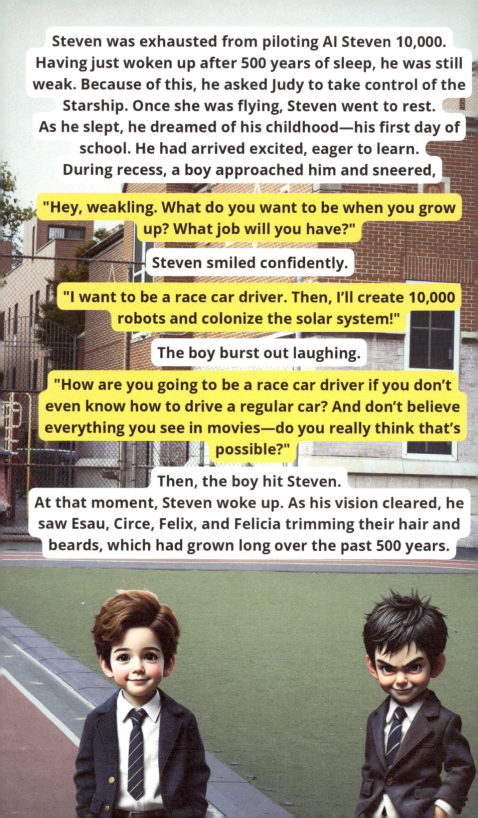

Steven was exhausted from piloting AI Steven 10,000. Having just woken up after 500 years of sleep, he was still weak. Because of this, he asked Judy to take control of the Starship. Once she was flying, Steven went to rest.
As he slept, he dreamed of his childhood—his first day of school. He had arrived excited, eager to learn.
During recess, a boy approached him and sneered,

"Hey, weakling. What do you want to be when you grow up? What job will you have?"

Steven smiled confidently.

"I want to be a race car driver. Then, I'll create 10,000 robots and colonize the solar system!"

The boy burst out laughing.

"How are you going to be a race car driver if you don't even know how to drive a regular car? And don't believe everything you see in movies—do you really think that's possible?"

Then, the boy hit Steven.
At that moment, Steven woke up. As his vision cleared, he saw Esau, Circe, Felix, and Felicia trimming their hair and beards, which had grown long over the past 500 years.

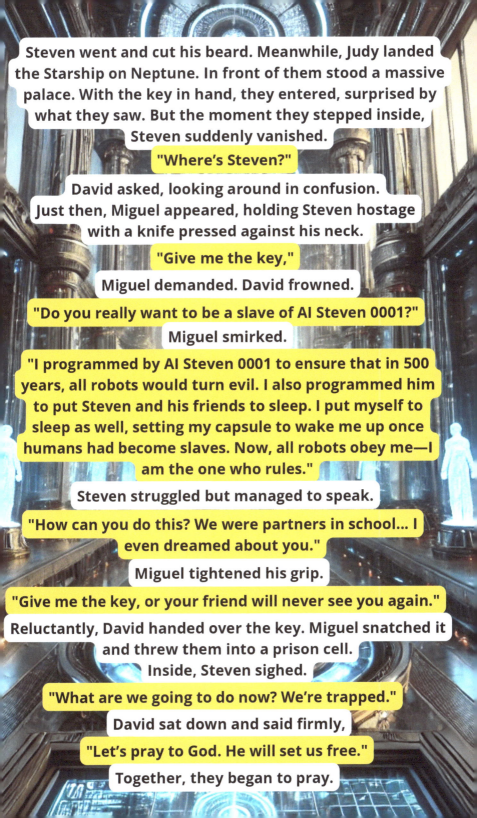

Steven went and cut his beard. Meanwhile, Judy landed the Starship on Neptune. In front of them stood a massive palace. With the key in hand, they entered, surprised by what they saw. But the moment they stepped inside, Steven suddenly vanished.

"Where's Steven?"

David asked, looking around in confusion. Just then, Miguel appeared, holding Steven hostage with a knife pressed against his neck.

"Give me the key,"

Miguel demanded. David frowned.

"Do you really want to be a slave of AI Steven 0001?"

Miguel smirked.

"I programmed by AI Steven 0001 to ensure that in 500 years, all robots would turn evil. I also programmed him to put Steven and his friends to sleep. I put myself to sleep as well, setting my capsule to wake me up once humans had become slaves. Now, all robots obey me—I am the one who rules."

Steven struggled but managed to speak.

"How can you do this? We were partners in school... I even dreamed about you."

Miguel tightened his grip.

"Give me the key, or your friend will never see you again."

Reluctantly, David handed over the key. Miguel snatched it and threw them into a prison cell. Inside, Steven sighed.

"What are we going to do now? We're trapped."

David sat down and said firmly,

"Let's pray to God. He will set us free."

Together, they began to pray.

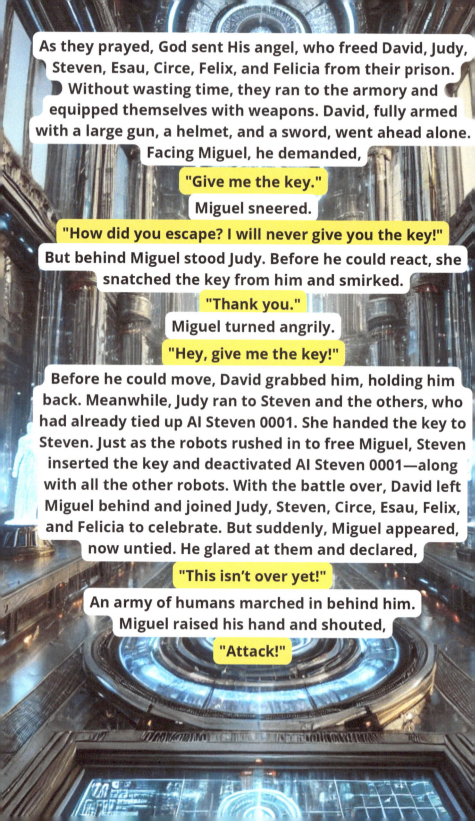

As they prayed, God sent His angel, who freed David, Judy, Steven, Esau, Circe, Felix, and Felicia from their prison. Without wasting time, they ran to the armory and equipped themselves with weapons. David, fully armed with a large gun, a helmet, and a sword, went ahead alone. Facing Miguel, he demanded,

"Give me the key."

Miguel sneered.

"How did you escape? I will never give you the key!"

But behind Miguel stood Judy. Before he could react, she snatched the key from him and smirked.

"Thank you."

Miguel turned angrily.

"Hey, give me the key!"

Before he could move, David grabbed him, holding him back. Meanwhile, Judy ran to Steven and the others, who had already tied up AI Steven 0001. She handed the key to Steven. Just as the robots rushed in to free Miguel, Steven inserted the key and deactivated AI Steven 0001—along with all the other robots. With the battle over, David left Miguel behind and joined Judy, Steven, Circe, Esau, Felix, and Felicia to celebrate. But suddenly, Miguel appeared, now untied. He glared at them and declared,

"This isn't over yet!"

An army of humans marched in behind him. Miguel raised his hand and shouted,

"Attack!"

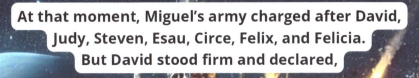

At that moment, Miguel's army charged after David, Judy, Steven, Esau, Circe, Felix, and Felicia. But David stood firm and declared,

"The Lord fights for us!"

With renewed strength, they fought back. Suddenly, a vast army of angels descended from the heavens and attacked Miguel's forces. Seeing his defeat, Miguel turned and ran suspiciously. David, determined not to let him escape, pursued him. As David caught up, he saw massive pipes running from the castle to the colony. Miguel, grinning wickedly, said,

"These pipes will transport lava and destroy the colony. If I can't rule humanity, then I will rule the robots!"

Before Miguel could act, Steven appeared behind him and thrust a sword through his back. Steven turned to David and said,

"I'll order the army to evacuate the castle. You're a plumber, right? This is your moment."

David rushed to a nearby computer and reprogrammed the pipes, redirecting the lava flow back toward the castle. As soon as Miguel's army was the only one left inside, David ran out. Moments later, the castle exploded into flames.

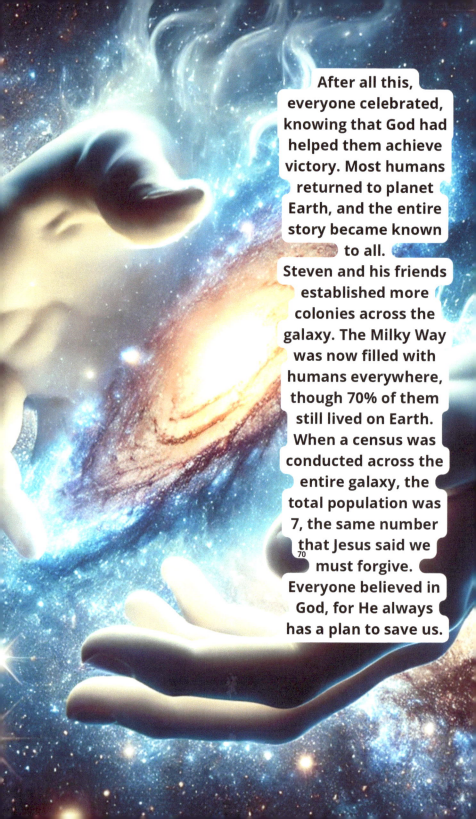

After all this, everyone celebrated, knowing that God had helped them achieve victory. Most humans returned to planet Earth, and the entire story became known to all.

Steven and his friends established more colonies across the galaxy. The Milky Way was now filled with humans everywhere, though 70% of them still lived on Earth. When a census was conducted across the entire galaxy, the total population was 7, the same number that Jesus said we must forgive. Everyone believed in God, for He always has a plan to save us.

70

Draw Your Own Character

David

Judy

Steven

Esau

Circe

Felix

Felicia

Notes

What was your favorite part of this book?

_____

Which page did you like the most?

_____

_____

Who was your favorite character?

_____

_____

_____

_____

_____

_____